ALLEN PHOTOGRAPHIC GUIDES

RIN

D1586809

CONTENTS

WHAT IS RINGCRAFT?

Ringcraft is the art of pre-senting your show animal in the ring and affording him the greatest possible chance of impressing the judge.

Showing is about creating the best picture and making an instant impact. As well as emphasising the pony's good points it is important to know, and to try to improve and cover up, his weaknesses, for example, if your animal has a bad trot then it is common sense not to labour this gait.

By observing the experts who have per-fected their craft, you can add to your knowledge. Watch how they can transform an average exhibit into a champion and make a real star almost unbeatable. Never be afraid to ask advice from these people if you are having problems as they have years of experience on which to draw.

WHAT THE JUDGE IS LOOKING FOR

Unlike racing where the first past the post wins, the outcome of a show class depends entirely on the judge's opinion which is founded on a sound knowledge of the requirements of each class.

The show ring is a place of great interest and speculation because judges place differing emphasis on criteria such as type, correctness of conformation, way of going and manners.

Today it is essential to have a pony of the correct type in order to win at top level shows as standards are so high. It is unlikely that a top-class show hunter pony could win a show pony class at a county show. Type is very closely related to conformation as it defines the specific role of the animal, i.e. a thoroughbred is built for speed and a shire for strength.

In theory a pony with good, well-balanced conformation will not only please the eye but should also be able to perform more efficiently, be more comfortable to ride and, consequently, remain sound.

Quality is essential in the show animal and is defined as overall refinement and class. It does not mean weedy and light of limb, which is a fault.

AUTHOR'S TIP

Tuning in to what a judge might like is important. There is little point travelling hundreds of miles to a show in the knowledge that the judge is not enamoured of your pony. The animal's success depends on your ability to place him under judges who will appreciate his qualities. Also, take note of which judges may not be able to judge your pony due to some connection with him in the past, possibly as a trainer or breeder.

Presence is that extra something which catches the judge's eye; a pony saying 'look at me' stands out from the crowd. Presence is the animal's personality showing through and usually develops as the animal becomes more confident and happier in his work. Without presence the animal will appear automated and his performance will leave little impression on the judge.

In addition, ponies should be well mannered in the ring so a good temperament is an essential part of a competition animal's make up.

TYPES OF PONY

Show Pony The show pony is the epitome of beauty and elegance, like the show hack but with pony characteristics. Certain ponies may appear to have plain heads and slightly more substance than others (sooner this than a bad hind leg or odd-shaped feet) but they are still show ponies as they do not possess either the limb or workmanlike qualities of the hunter pony. The show pony can be likened to a catwalk model, both must be seemingly flawless and a delight to watch because of their graceful movement.

Both lead-rein and first-ridden ponies must be absolutely safe. They should possess a good front, even gaits and not be too wide for their small jockeys. The stride should not be too long as this would unseat the rider and cause him to lose his balance. Ideally the first-ridden pony is a little more scopey in both conformation and movement than the lead-rein pony although many ponies compete successfully in both classes.

The 12.2 hh show pony, like its lead-rein/first-ridden counterparts, may show some native breeding but on the whole should have more quality and a more elegant way of going.

In general the 13.2 hh pony is the model pattern as its breeding is less influenced by the native pony than the 12.2 hh pony. Many 14.2 hh ponies have thoroughbred in their bloodlines to get the height and, as a result, sometimes look a little stronger and more horsy (see right).

Show Hunter Pony If the show pony is described as pretty and charming, then the show hunter pony must be a miniature hunter possessing the quality, substance and conformation which would enable him to perform his duties soundly in the hunting field. His gaits are more workmanlike than those of the show pony because too much elevation or grace would render him useless in heavy going, particularly at the gallop. His conformation must also reflect his role, i.e. a deep girth, sound limbs and short cannons with good flat bone sufficient to carry his frame.

Working Hunter Pony Ideally the working hunter pony should be a show hunter pony who can jump. However, as the name suggests, he can afford to be slightly plainer than his show counterpart and may also have a few battle scars as he has a more demanding role to perform.

Intermediates These classes for show, hunter and working types are meant as a stepping stone into the adult classes for the young riders and consequently require a hack/riding horse, small hunter and small working hunter respectively (see below). Intermediate animals must be capable of competing successfully in adult classes and not just be misfits that do not slot into any particular class.

Novice Pony It is important that the novice pony goes happily in a snaffle bridle. Although he is not expected to look or perform as maturely as the animals in the open classes, he must still behave because it is in these classes that he learns about showing.

Matching the rider to the pony is essential to create the right picture. From a judge's point of view, a large jockey can cover up a quality pony and a tiny jockey may not only look overhorsed but can also make a pony seem plainer.

AUTHOR'S TIP

With any young animal you must be prepared to take plenty of time to educate him. Taking him to shows and riding him round is a good idea as it gives you an accurate impression of his reactions at a show as well as giving you an indication as to how much work he would require when showing.

PREPARATION AT THE SHOW

USE OF TIME

Always make sure you have allowed yourself enough time to get to the show as there is nothing worse than trying to do things when in a flap. Take notice of traffic reports and set off early enough, especially on Bank Holidays and times when the roads are busy. Certain shows are near busy towns and quite often you can be caught up in the morning rush hour which can cause considerable delays.

When you arrive collect your numbers from the secretary (if necessary) and check on the final timetable as there may have been a last minute change of ring, time or judge. You may also have to declare your intention to compete.

Look at the ring to see if there is anything around it that your pony may not like and you would wish to avoid – although your pony should be well trained enough not to misbehave –

you still do not want to court disaster. Make a note of whether the ring is flat or not as you will not want to change the rein or gallop downhill if you can avoid it.

Familiarise yourself with the showground layout as, with the advent of horsewalks, it can sometimes take you twice as long to get to the ring.

AUTHOR'S TIP

If you are late for your class by only a couple of minutes, then it is polite to approach the steward to apologise and ask to join the others rather than sneak in. Some societies have specific rules regarding this situation.

WALKING THE COURSE

For working hunter pony classes you will need to walk the course; ensure you check with the steward that it is the right one as tracks are often altered for different classes. Again, look for the best ground and think about what line you will take between fences to give your pony the best chance of a clear round.

Understand what the course builder is trying to achieve and locate danger areas, i.e. by the entrance, any tight turns etc. Walk the exact track you intend to ride, memorising the course and double checking your line by looking back towards the fence. You can use markers – flag poles for example – to help you to ride a straight line through fences, particularly if they are offset.

WORKING IN

Always give yourself plenty of time to work a pony in; you may think that he has had enough work but then something could unsettle him and you will have to go back to square one. Once you find a programme which works, stick to it because ponies thrive on routine.

> **AUTHOR'S TIP**
>
> If your animal is young and inexperienced try to find a quiet corner where he will concentrate on his work without the distractions of other ponies and only when he is settled take him to a busier area.

If the ground is particularly hard or space limited, hacking him around will allow him to absorb the atmosphere and settle down. If he is particularly fresh then lungeing may help. We tend to lunge in a cavesson so that the pony can warm up without being restricted by side reins etc. As young ponies quite often buck and spook when they first come out of the box, wearing tight side reins would inhibit their balance and may result in them slipping and falling over.

COLLECTING RING

It is imperative to make your way to the collecting ring on time so that you are able to compose yourself and enter the ring unflustered. Once in the collecting ring, give your pony sufficient work to settle him or, if he is in the right frame of mind, just walk round. If you are in the following class, watch where the judge has lined the ponies up and if there is not a set show then plan what to do.

In the case of working hunter ponies you may want to watch a couple of rounds to see how the course is jumping before doing your final warm up and jumping the practice fence. This is also the time for last minute checks such as girth, keepers on bridles, removing the tail bandage and giving the pony a final wipe over.

IN THE RING

The object of showing your pony is to impress the judge so that, hopefully, you will win a rosette. It is crucial, therefore, that you present your pony at his best whenever the judge is looking at you. We like to think of the ring as a stage: the long side is the front of the stage whilst the other three sides are the wings where the rider prepares the pony for his appearance along the front. Consequently, it can be annoying when a judge keeps turning round as you never quite know where they are looking!

Quite often you see overzealous adults leading animals into the ring – this is against British Show Pony Society rules and is totally unnecessary. Should your pony hang back, let a few animals go before you so that he has a lead. Similarly if there are a few animals bunched around the entrance to the ring, let them go first so that you can walk straight in and not get involved in a scrum. As you enter the ring, try to place yourself between inferior animals so that your pony looks better and avoid getting behind a pony with a poor walk because this will hold you up and spoil the appearance of your pony's walk.

THE WALK

As it is the first and last gait that the judge sees it is very important that your pony walks forward properly, tracking-up well without shortening his stride and twisting away from your leg. He needs to be purposeful and alert but relaxed, walking over the ground rather than into it. It is essential that you maintain a space both in front and behind you so that your animal can move without getting too close to the animal in front and avoid being pushed along by someone too close behind you. It is rather like driving a car: you not only have to watch what you are doing but also make allowances for other people's miscalculations in order to avoid problems.

THE TROT

After you have completed your first circuit, glance at the steward to ascertain when he may ask you to trot; when he does, ride your pony into an even flowing rhythm covering the ground well. One of the worst sights is seeing a pony trotting so fast that he lands on his heel instead of his toe with no natural rhythm. By-pass anything that may alarm your pony as the ring is not the place for a confrontation. Again, keep an eye on the steward so that you will be able to prepare for canter in plenty of time.

AUTHOR'S TIP

A good judge will find a good pony but you can make it easier for him by keeping in a space; it is up to you to be on the ball and make sure that you are seen. This is a particular problem if there are a lot of animals in the ring as bunching can occur.

How to find a space:
1. Overtake and find a suitable gap elsewhere.
2. Circle into a space behind where you were.

Both these solutions should not be performed in front of the judge as they could obstruct his view of other ponies.

3. By going deeper into the corners giving yourself more room.

THE CANTER

It is a good idea, especially with a novice, to use the corner to help put him on the correct leg in canter and ask for the transition quietly so that the canter is not rushed. Learn to feel for the correct lead rather than looking down as this tends to upset the pony's balance and will actually cause him to drop onto the wrong leg thus defeating the object. If you do strike off on the wrong leg, try not to become flustered, come down to a nice steady trot and wait for the next corner or circle him before asking for canter again. The canter should be smooth, flowing and balanced, showing self-carriage.

Never allow the stride to shorten or 'motorbike' around corners.

CHANGING THE REIN

You will then be asked to change the rein, usually performed at trot although some judges prefer to bring the class to a walk. Work out which track you will take well in advance and ride your pony into a steady, even trot before going across the diagonal.

The judge may sometimes use this to see how straight the animals move so your pony should be going in a straight line, not too fast or he will be on his forehand and unbalanced. If he doesn't move particularly straight then try to avoid heading directly for the judge.

Be especially careful with a nervous pony when changing the rein as ponies coming towards him may upset him. If this is the case, try to get in the middle order of ponies across the diagonal so that, by the time he returns to the track, all the others will also have changed and he should not, therefore, meet anything head on.

Once you have changed the rein return to canter as indicated by the steward.

THE GALLOP

When galloping as a class, being in a good space is important because animals coming up too close to you or even overtaking may cause your pony to buck. If he is lazy then it may help if you get a lead from another pony. On the other hand, if he is sharp try to be one of the first to gallop (this also applies when galloping four at a time). Once you have a space, prepare your animal

so that he can accelerate smoothly out of the corner showing a proper lengthening and lowering of the stride. So often riders canter slowly into the corner and then suddenly attack their ponies with heels and elbows flying. This not only produces an untidy scurry up the long side but also encourages the animal to fall in on the corner and thus drop onto his forehand; in this position he is far more likely to buck and mar his performance.

When you are three-quarters of the way along the long side, start to ease your pony back to a canter so that he is balanced by the time he reaches the corner. If you leave it too late to pull up, momentum takes over which may cause him to slip and fall in the corner (this would result in you having to retire from the class).

In contrast some jockeys ride their gallop rather half-heartedly and only push their

ponies up to halfway along the side resulting in a feeble display.

> ### AUTHOR'S TIP
>
> Although there is no better feeling than riding an animal which can really gallop well, never overdo it (especially on hard ground) when working in or after a completed jumping round, for example. You may soon develop problems as your pony begins to anticipate this gait.

After the canter (or gallop), the steward will bring the class back to walk so that the judge can make his selection. It is your last chance to be noticed at this stage of the proceedings so make sure, therefore, that your pony is concentrating on his job and at the same time keep an eye on the steward (without staring) so that you do not miss your pull in. (The same applies to the final walk round at the end of the class.) If you are not pulled in early then do not become despondent and allow things to fall apart, there is still a long way to go before the rosettes are presented so you must redouble your efforts and produce a good show.

COMING OUT OF LINE

If there is the possibility that your pony might nap coming out of line then practise riding him away on his own at home; napping in the ring is usually caused by a lack of obedience in the first place. Also, give yourself plenty of time to stand him up for the judge if you know that he may be unwilling to come out of line. If, on the contrary, he is likely to fidget when waiting for the judge then leave coming out of line as late as possible. Whilst the judge is looking over your pony make sure he is alert (see above), not resting a hind leg or falling asleep. However, do not be tempted to hold his head in as he will not only look uncomfortable and forced, but will also probably fidget.

AUTHOR'S TIP

It is imperative to teach your pony to halt and stand properly as halt is not only required at the beginning and end of the show but also long periods of time are spent waiting in line. At home we tend to halt on the track when we have finished work and then walk forward on a long rein. If you need to recreate the conditions under which your pony will not stand, then stopping in the entrance of the school facing towards home and waiting two or three minutes before walking on may help. If he continues to be disobedient, then keep halting all the way back to the stables and pat him when he performs it well.

JUMPING THE WORKING HUNTER PONY

On entering the ring, walk or trot smartly towards the judge. Halt and after saying 'good morning/afternoon' give him your number. The judge will then signal you to start either verbally or with a whistle. Settle into a working canter as soon as possible, rather than circling endlessly, and focus your pony's attention on the job in hand. This will give an impression of efficiency to the judge and set the tone for the round. As you ride your course concentrate only on the approaching fence and, once you have landed, ride for the next fence and so on. Look ahead and keep to your planned route,

maintaining an even, balanced rhythm so that you can present your animal correctly for each fence. This will not only earn you valuable style marks but will also prevent a build-up of speed. In general you will need to ride steadily into uprights and more forward for parallels.

If you do have a problem at a fence, stay calm and keep thinking rather than panicking and falling apart. After you have completed the course bring your pony to a steady trot and then leave the ring at walk. (You may need to return to the judge and salute.) You should never leave the ring at a flat-out gallop.

After jumping you may have to go straight into another ring for the show and conformation phase if there are two judges. However, more often than not, you will have to wait until all the rounds have been jumped in your height section and then wait to see if you are required. Usually all clear rounds return although, if there have

not been many, knock downs and refusals will also be needed.

SHOWING INDOORS

Indoor shows have an atmosphere of their own, so practising in a local arena will be useful before venturing to a show. Most of the purpose-built, modern indoor schools are quite big and light but still require a good deal of concentration to ride in them. Sounds echo far more and most animals take a little time to get used to a gallery with people moving around in it. Use your corners to make space as you ride around the ring and avoid getting too close to the pony in front as the surface may kick up into your animal's face and spook him.

Depending on the size of class, you may be lined up along the centre line or across the short end of the school, which will require some quick planning if there is not a set show.

THE INDIVIDUAL SHOW

The individual show is your opportunity to impress the judge. You have their sole attention for two or three minutes so make the most of it by using your common sense. Unless it is set, vary a basic show (see Fig. 1 on page 16) to show off your pony's best points. If he has an exceptional trot you should perform an extra trot and finish the show with a good trot (see Fig. 2 on page 16). If he isn't impressive at

trot but does move straight, trot across the diagonal (see Fig. 3 on page 16) rather than along the front. If your forte is canter, a two-change would be better (see Fig. 4 on page 16). If you have a problem riding onto the correct lead in right canter then design your show so that you canter left first and then the pony will more often than not find the right leg on the change of rein. If your pony anticipates his show, do something different every time. If you are required to ride a circle keep it even. The most important thing to remember is that the show should be accurate and fluent. You may need to alter your planned show halfway through because you break into canter unexpectedly or a tractor decides to unload some straw bales at the side of the ring. If you are given a set show and are not quite sure what to do, ask the steward to tell you again so that you get it right. Occasionally you may have to perform shows in pairs, whenever possible liaise with the other rider so as to avoid complications and crashes.

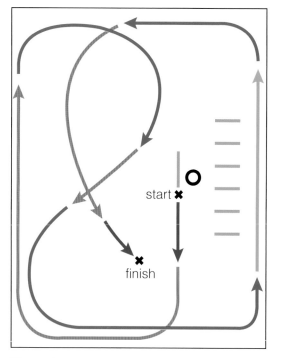

Figure 1

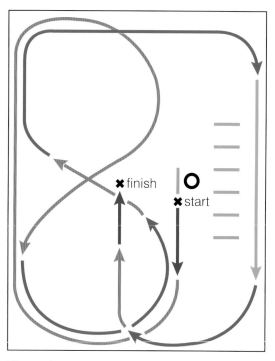

Figure 2

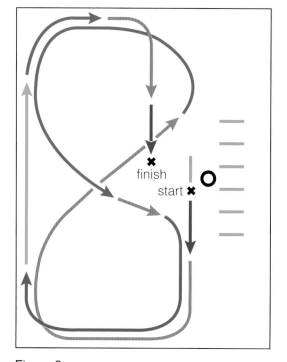

Figure 3

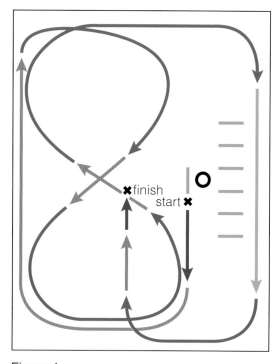

Figure 4

halt —— walk ▬▬ trot ▬▬▬ canter —— gallop —— O judge

INTERMEDIATE CLASSES

In Intermediate classes where exhibitors are more adult, a serpentine, rein-back or walk to canter may be included but only if it can be performed with panache, if you are not confident then keep your show simple.

THE HALT

It is important that you ride your halt properly. You cannot pull on the reins and expect a correct halt – always ride him into it with your seat and leg and then he will stand square ready to move off. With a fidgety pony you may be better facing the line-up when halting at the end of the show so that he can see the other ponies. Similarly if you are required to rein-back, halting by the side of the ring will help to keep you straight.

THE REIN-BACK

The rein-back should be an even, regular two-time gait performed from a square halt. If the pony does not relax into his halt, then his rein-back will be tense and have an irregular rhythm and will probably skew to one side, which will be particularly obvious if the judge stands directly in front of or behind you.

LEAD-REIN SHOWS (see Fig. 5 above)

These are becoming more testing now as the standard of this class improves although the judge is still looking for the same basic requirements. Transitions should be smooth with no sudden movements and the stride should be even to accommodate a small rider's abilities. It is important to maintain a flowing rhythm especially on the turns with the pony having a steady head carriage so

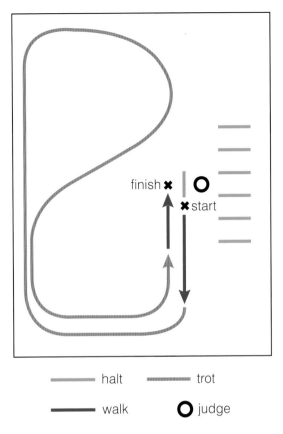

finish ✗   O

✗ start

halt ▭▭▭ trot ▭▭▭

walk ▬▬▬ O judge

Figure 5

that the jockey is not being pulled out of the saddle.

Ideally the handler should keep alongside providing security for the rider but not interfering directly with the pony (see top photo on page 18). The handler should not dominate the picture by keeping a tight hold of the pony and seeming to do all the work, almost as if showing the pony in an in-hand class. However, at the other end of the scale, some handlers, in an attempt to give a totally independent picture, leave the rein dangling by the pony's feet (see centre photo on page 18) or lead so far away they appear to be lungeing him (see bottom photo on page 18).

POINTS TO REMEMBER

1. Always do exactly what the judge/steward tells you.

2. Use the ring space well and keep some sort of pattern.

3. Gauge the time of your show; shows that are rushed, particularly at the end, and those that go on and on, will not impress the judge.

4. Smooth transitions are important especially through the change of rein. Trot for about four or five strides in your change of rein, neither breaking into trot too early or, worse still, using the ringside to bring your pony back to trot.

5. Keep your circles symmetrical in the figure-of-eight; a common mistake is to make a big circle in the first part of the figure, leaving it tight for the second half.

6. If you start your show as the previous competitor is finishing theirs, make sure the judge is watching you.

7. Avoid galloping downhill in case the pony becomes unbalanced and bucks.

Ideally the peak of the gallop should be behind the line up. It is better to take time to build up to a good gallop than charge off too early and then 'run out of petrol' at the end.

8. Finish your show well; make sure that the downward transitions are timed well, not out of control and then finishing with a sudden halt. Do not halt far away from the judge, and acknowledge them without performing a salute like an Elizabethan courtier.

9. **Look as though you are enjoying yourself!**

THE IN-HAND SHOW

You may be required to unsaddle your pony for the in-hand phase, so make sure that you have someone with you who can perform this task and tidy up the pony so that he looks a picture when in front of the judge. The assistant should be smartly turned out, wearing a hat, and have the right equipment for the weather conditions. It is a good idea to take a bucket of water to wash muddy legs off on a wet day when waterproofs for horse and rider may be needed as well. All rugs should have fillet strings attached to prevent them being blown about and frightening the animal. On a hot day, drinks for the rider are a good idea and the pony's fly repellent might need to be reapplied.

In-hand shows are an often-neglected area where ponies can make up points in the eyes of a judge. Come out of line smartly, do not drag your pony because he has fallen asleep in line or is napping. Again, practise at home getting just the right stance for your animal. Some need to

look up to give the impression of a more swan-like front but, if your pony lacks length of rein, he will need to stretch a little and keep his head lower.

A common mistake is to throw grass into the air in an effort to try to catch the pony's attention and get him to prick his ears forward. More often than not, the animal looks startled instead and raises his head which results in his back hollowing and the muscle under his neck being emphasised. Try to stand on a good piece of level ground or slightly uphill, never downhill, facing the direction you intend to walk away from the judge. Stand in front of the pony so as to give the judge a clear view of him and keep his attention so that he stands quietly. If the judge is looking at him from the nearside, have the nearside foreleg slightly in front of the offside one and the nearside hind leg slightly behind the offside one thereby framing the picture. When the judge moves round to the other side, reverse these positions either by moving a stride forward or backward. Do not let your animal splay out like a hackney or stand 'in a heap' as both these positions will detract from the overall impression. Make sure that the animal is standing square (see opposite top left), so that when viewed from in front or behind, his legs are not twisted giving a bad impression of his conformation. This often happens when the pony is halted whilst still turning.

Remember to walk away in even strides on a straight line (see top right) using a marker such as a trade stand, if necessary, then go left off the track on a small half-circle to return on your original line. When your pony is straight, go into a nice steady trot towards the judge, keeping the line, so that he can determine (see bottom left) whether your pony moves straight. Two common faults are turning the pony too tightly on the turn and starting to trot while on the turn, both of which can cause the pony to catch himself and possibly go lame. Also, not trotting straight toward the judge makes his job more difficult and can annoy him (see bottom right). If your pony is reluctant to trot-up, prime your groom to discreetly shake a cloth or something to help you. On the other hand, if your animal is sharp do not trot too fast otherwise he may break into canter.

After you have trotted past the judge, carry on round the ring and back into your place in line, then your groom will tack up the pony again and get you back on board. Once on your pony you may need to have a little walk round before returning to the line-up to relax him. At this stage keep the pony alert as the judge may cast a glance over the class before making his final assessment. You may also have to ride a final walk round so your pony must look his best.

A good showman will have flicked the flap of his jacket over the back of the saddle and slipped the loop of the reins to the nearside to make the picture as tidy as possible. Giving the pony an occasional pat also gives a confident and professional look.

All is over when the steward dismisses the class but you are still on show and the lap of honour should be done properly. If your pony becomes excited then settling him first in trot is a good idea. We always ask our jockeys to come back to a walk before they leave the ring so that the pony exits under control and calmly, otherwise he thinks it is just part of a mad dash back to the box and his haynet!

AFTER THE CLASS

HANDLING THE PRESS

Take the time to stand your pony up well for the press photographer and have interesting details of the pony's breeding and previous results to hand for the reporter as he will probably be short of time and making the effort guarantees an accurate report. This information may also be required if you are involved in a grand parade.

As soon as you have finished your day's showing unplait the pony as leaving plaits in may cause him to rub and break his mane. If you are showing the next day, however, you may want to leave them in. Old stockings held in place with plaiting bands or a Lycra hood may be useful but it depends on the individual concerned. Ponies who roll a lot will get bedding ingrained in their manes and, especially in the case of shavings, it may be extremely difficult to remove.

Any make-up or fly repellent must be wiped off and sweat marks brushed or sponged off before bandaging and rugging up. Offer your pony a drink before setting off, especially if you have a long journey.

It is important always to analyse your performance and have a postmortem at home. If you have gone well and won, do not become too complacent but look at areas in which you can still improve. If you have had a bad day, try to be positive and look at how to get round whatever problems you are experiencing, perhaps arrange for some lessons from a more experienced person or ask the advice of a knowledgeable fellow exhibitor. Be objective and try to improve your performance and presentation, persuading a friend to film you and your pony on a video camera may help.

ACKNOWLEDGEMENTS

The authors wish to express their sincere thanks to Penny Hollings and photographer Chris Cook, for their help in the preparation of this book.

British Library Cataloguing-in-Publication Data.
A catalogue record for this book is available from the
British Library

ISBN 0.85131.711.1

Published in Great Britain in 1998 by
J. A. Allen & Company Limited,
1 Lower Grosvenor Place, Buckingham Palace Road,
London, SW1W OEL

Design and Typesetting by Paul Saunders
Series editor Jane Lake
Colour Separation by Tenon & Polert (H.K.) Ltd
Printed in Hong Kong by Dah Hua Printing Press Co. Ltd.